Adrian van Kaam

with a Foreword by **Susan Muto**

The Tender Farewell of Jesus

Meditations on Chapter 17 of John's Gospel

New City Press

The Tender Farewell of Jesus

Published in the United States by New City Press
202 Cardinal Rd., Hyde Park, NY 12538
©1996 Epiphany Association

Cover design by Nick Cianfarani
Cover art from Christ Church Cathedral, 1832.

Bible quotations are from The Jerusalem Bible ©1986 by Darton, Long-
man and Todd, Ltd. and Doubleday & Company, Inc. Used by permis-
sion of the publisher.

Library of Congress Cataloging-in-Publication Data:

Van Kaam, Adrian L., 1920-
    The tender farewell of Jesus : meditations on chapter 17 of John's
Gospel / Adrian van Kaam : with a foreword by Susan Muto.
        p.   cm.
    ISBN 1-56548-080-5 (pbk.)
    1. Bible.   N.T.   John XVII—Meditations.   I. Title.
BS2615.4.V37   1996
226.5'06—dc20   96-25780
                                                    CIP

Printed in the United States of America

Contents

The Tender Farewell of Jesus

At his last supper
Jesus leaves us his testament:
A chant of love, a song of intimacy
With Trinity and humanity;
A dance of consonance with all that is;
A hymn of praise to the Father;
A tender farewell
To us his loved ones.
To live this love
Is to long for the paradise
Of intimacy Divine.

Adrian van Kaam

Foreword

This lovely book of meditations on Jesus' farewell prayer in the Gospel of John has to be read with the eyes of the heart. We have to picture the touching scene of parting with all its sweet sorrow. Jesus loved life. He wanted us to live it to the full. He knew that true prayer comes when we are so full of love for others and for God that we cannot contain it. Then to pray is to pray through the power of the Holy Spirit.

This is what happened to Jesus when he met with his beloved friends and disciples to offer them the legacy of his last words. Every phrase of the farewell prayer is laden with love, overflowing with lessons to be learned and good example to be set.

The text has a surplus of meaning no amount of reading could exhaust. The wonder of this book is that Adrian van Kaam taps into its potential to both inform our understanding and transform our relationship to the Lord. He writes as if he were on the scene, overhearing Jesus' message, ruminating on its meaning for the sake of helping us to seek God and serve others. When prose fails to contain the depth dimension of Christ's prayer, Father Adrian himself becomes a poet, praying with Jesus in songs of longing love that take us to a new level of contemplation. We not only grasp the inmost depth of Jesus' message; we feel it in our bones. We want to live it more faithfully day to day.

Underlying these meditations as a whole—at least according to my reading—are three intertwining themes: *abandonment to the providential plan of God* (believing the word of the Lord, even when, humanly speaking, we do not see or understand its outcome); *becoming conscious of the personal and social profile of sin that threatens at every turn to block this plan* (the self-centeredness that prevents us from being God-centered, the inner and outer conflicts that preclude peace and kill joy); and *growing daily in the conviction that without God we are and can do nothing* (the humble acknowledgment of our complete dependence on the Divine for everything).

Jesus himself was the abandoned one. Already from childhood the whole of his life could be contained in one phrase: "Yes, Father. Your will, not mine, be done." He showed his disciples by word and deed that God's strong arm upholds us when we take the leap of faith, let go of our preset agendas, and follow the narrow way that leads to abundant life.

Abandonment or self-renunciation leads, as Jesus tells his disciples, to freedom or liberation to go where God leads, even if this is the way of the cross. When felt consolations subside, naked faith begins. Only in total abandonment is the absolute breaking of the chain of sin and death possible. At the heart of the abandoned soul, paradox abounds: Perfect love casts out fear; joy overtakes sorrow; rays of glory stream from Jesus' outstretched arms.

With gentleness and firmness, Jesus makes us attentive to the subtle forms sin takes. Before we know it we choose self-interest over serving others. We betray our friends and conform to the ways of the world. We refuse to be peacemakers, and instead lose ourselves in endless bickering, one-upmanship, and joyless judgmentalism. More serious than any of these sins is our lack of trust in the Holy Spirit, the advocate Jesus sends to plea for us and to pray for us in sighs and groans too deep for words. Sinners though we are, we refuse to rely on the power of our Savior's mercy and forgiveness. We make the cardinal mistake of thinking we can be self-reliant.

It is this message that the farewell prayer of Jesus drives home. Jesus is the vine; we are the branches. He is the master; we are his disciples. Our lives must grow in reliance on him and in conformity to the Father's will. He wants us to know that we are not alone. We have a friend in Jesus, a lover willing to lay down his life for us. Nothing hurts Jesus more than when we forget to ask him for what we need, when we pretend that we can do it alone. That is why he asks us to love one another as he has loved us. He wants us to rely on one another, to be a community of faith, and to offer our brothers and sisters everywhere a message of hope, a hand of peace.

Adrian van Kaam has not only given us a superb commentary on Jesus' hymn of love; he has also read between the lines of Jesus' teaching to capture its transformative power. People of all ages seek solid food to nourish their spiritual hunger. They want the assurance that when they let go of their "control-center-me" mentality and appreciatively abandon themselves to God's guidance, all shall be well. No one can find peace without the promise of forgiveness Jesus gives, without the mercy and compassion he shows us sinners. And all of us need to know that depending on God is the key to what Father Adrian calls in another book of his, "our holy fecundity in world and history."

The Tender Farewell of Jesus is a storehouse of wisdom and truth. It is a book to be read and reread with the expectation that new treasures of insight and meaning await us each time. Father Adrian's original poems lead us to prayer and to a renewed commitment to bear fruit that will last. In the end he convinces us that Jesus' farewell marks the start of our own mature formation in faith, hope, and love.

Susan Muto

Introduction

The Love Song of Jesus in the Gospel of John

John 17:1-23

After saying this, Jesus raised his eyes to
heaven and said:

Father, the hour has come;
glorify your Son
so that your Son may glorify you;
so that, just as you have given him power over
      all humanity,
he may give eternal life to all those you have
      entrusted to him.
And eternal life is this:
to know you,
the only true God,
and Jesus Christ whom you have sent.
I have glorified you on earth
by finishing the work
that you gave me to do.
Now, Father, glorify me
with that glory I had with you
before ever the world existed.
I have revealed your name
to those whom you took from the world to give
      me.

They were yours and you gave them to me,
and they have kept your word.
Now at last they have recognized
that all you have given me comes from you
for I have given them
the teaching you gave to me,
and they have indeed accepted it
and know for certain that I came from you,
and have believed that it was you who sent me.
It is for them that I pray.
I am not praying for the world
but for those you have given me,
because they belong to you.
All I have is yours,
and all you have is mine,
and in them I am glorified.
I am no longer in the world,
but they are in the world,
and I am coming to you.
Holy Father,
keep those you have given me true to your name,
so that they may be one like us.
While I was with them,
I kept those you had given me true to your name.
I have watched over them and not one is lost
except one who was destined to be lost,
and this was to fulfill the scriptures.
But now I am coming to you
and I say these things in the world
to share my joy with them to the full.
I passed your word on to them,

and the world hated them,
because they belong to the world
no more than I belong to the world.
I am not asking you to remove them from the
    world,
but to protect them from the Evil One.
They do not belong to the world
any more than I belong to the world.
Consecrate them in the truth;
your word is truth.
As you sent me into the world,
I have sent them into the world,
and for their sake I consecrate myself
so that they too may be consecrated in truth.
I pray not only for these
but also for those who through
their teaching will come to believe in me.
May they all be one,
just as, Father, you are in me and I am in you,
so that they also may be in us,
so that the world may believe it was you who sent
    me.
I have given them the glory you gave to me,
that they may be one as we are one.
With me in them and you in me,
may they be so perfected in unity
that the world will recognize that it was you who
    sent me
and that you have loved them as you have loved
    me.

The seventeenth chapter of John's Gospel, the

farewell song of Jesus, has deeply touched my heart. I often read it meditatively as a complement to chapter 13 of Paul's first letter to the Corinthians. Tradition calls it "the hymn to love," because in it the saint exalts the love of Christ as the main forming power of his and our life.

Loving Divinely

Before turning my attention fully to Jesus' hymn of love, the source of meditation for this book, I want to say that Paul's hymn reminds me of our aspiration to give and receive the kind of love that is patient and kind, that does not boast and is never rude, that trusts and hopes and perseveres (cf. 1 Cor 13:4-7).

This ability to love divinely is the gift of the Spirit to our soul. Baptism transfigured us into the image of Christ. Infused in us then was the potency for love divine. God never meant for this dynamic principle to remain hidden in our soul. It was to be released into every aspect of our here and now experiential life, transforming all that we are and do into the living likeness of Christ. The sublime fruit of that transformation is the daily sacrifice of our life in service of God and our fellow human beings.

Just how we come, despite sin and selfishness, to make that sacrifice is the theme of Jesus' farewell prayer. If selfless love is the aim of our Christian life then self-giving is the means to attain it. Only with the grace of Christ can we enter upon this way of

inner and outer formation, reformation, and transformation. Conversion to Christ and the fullness of
love is a condition for our becoming a loving presence to others, a helpmate for their growth. As long
as we are inwardly deformed by lack of love for
ourselves, we shall be unable to love others.

As a Christian, if I cannot accept the gifts and limits
God allows in my life, I cannot appreciate the gifts and
limits of those with whom I live day by day. When pride
or self-centeredness prevails over love and self-giving, it
obscures the radiance of Jesus others ought to see in us.
Only he can conquer the devastations of selfishness that
kill self-donation. Only Jesus, our Divine Physician, can
cure the anxious, insecure condemnations and rash
judgments to which pride gives rise.

As we read and meditate upon Jesus' hymn of love
and what it asks of us, we begin to experience a
change in our attitude toward others. Jesus' love
begins to break through in our daily encounters with
people. We become less manipulative and demand-
ing. We are more willing to forgive and forget, more
ready to make ourselves available to help others
within the boundaries of our own life call.

Spiritual growth happens not only from within
but also from without in the loving relationships we
foster. Growing in the love of Christ implies an
incarnation of that love in person-to-person encounters. Christ's love has to permeate our interiority
and our interactions with others. It has to flow forth

from our soul like a fresh spring.

Love reaches its height when it inspires a total oblation of self to God and neighbor. At that moment the love of Christ radiates from us in selfless generosity.

Let us meditate on the marks of the selfless love of Jesus. Our beloved Lord offers his whole life for others. He lays it down so that they may grow like him in the love of the Father. His sacrifice of love for us is total. He gives himself up to death so we may escape the power of sin, the pride principle in our soul that pushes God's plan for us aside like so many scraps of paper. Jesus begs the Father to help us elude the deceptive world of self-exaltation. It surrounds us on all sides and tempts us to crave for power, pleasure, and possession as ultimate. Jesus asks his Father to defeat the divisive influence of the Evil One, who plays on our excessive need for vainglory. He wants our fallen humanity to share in his wondrous gift of life and in the Spirit that animates his giving.

To sacrifice ourselves with Jesus is not the same as making sacrifices only for our own and others' betterment in worldly pleasure and position. People sacrifice consumer goods to save more money. They give up going on vacation one year to afford a longer holiday the next. They forgo attending one social event to be seen at another.

Jesus' sacrifice has nothing to do with merely financial or functional gain. It is solely for the glory of the Father. Our sacrifice, too, must be in tune with the Father's word, with what he wants us to do, not only inwardly but also outwardly in the world he entrusts to our care.

Sacrifice of Private Glory

Our divine destiny will be disclosed to us gradually by the Holy Spirit. The Spirit speaks to us through all that God wants or permits in our lives. The sacrifice asked of us is not only the gift of our life at its end in time, but an oblation daily renewed. Surrender of self to the role we are called to play in the mystery of divine love is the sacrifice that slowly transforms humanity, world, and history.

Playing our part to heal the break between humankind and its Creator demands from us a special sacrifice, that of our search for private glory. We have to die to the principle of division that poisons humanity. If we are to share with others in the divine transformation of the world, we must participate in the self-giving love of the Son. God's direction for this world cannot be served as long as we do anything to contradict his designs.

Our role in the unfolding transformation of life and world by the Divine cannot be clear at once. This decision on our part to follow Christ, though we do not always know where we are being led, is another source of sacrificial living. No sooner do we settle down to one way of living then a new situation, an inner or outer change, presents itself.

Coming to yet another stage of maturation may reveal that where we are now is no longer the way meant for us by the Father. Unsettled though we may feel, we are being called to share in the prayer of praise of Jesus.

For the glory of the Father, we may have to let go of hitherto cherished customs, familiar surroundings, and facile popularity with family, friends, and colleagues. As we begin to change, thanks to the grace of God, we may become a question in others' minds. Our attempt to live more humbly and simply may offend the pride principle in them. With the suffering Christ, we may incur their condemnation.

Any life transition can evoke a crisis on many levels of experience—physical illness, emotional drain, spiritual dryness. By the same token, any transcendence crisis can be seen as a formation opportunity. It enables us to disclose with a little more clarity our unique participation in the mysterious life in Jesus to which the Father calls us. A transcendence crisis can also be a graced occasion to restore and deepen our participation in Jesus' redeeming sacrifice. It reminds us that our life is far from perfect. We are only on the road toward likeness with the sacrificial life of Jesus. We never arrive; we are always arriving.

What grounds our sharing in the daily oblation of Jesus' life is the spirit of prayer. The unfolding sacrifice of our life should be in service of the divine direction of history and humanity. It is pleasing to the Father when it is permeated by prayerful presence in and with Jesus to the needs of others entrusted to our care. Jesus' turning to the Father in his prayer of praise at the end of his life delights in that presence because his prayer is not one of gloom and sadness. On the contrary, it is filled with adoration and thanksgiving for his gifts to us and through us to others. Before he leaves the intimacy and protection of this last meal with his friends, he lifts his heart to the Father.

Final Intimate Words

What is to come is dreadfully near now. The setting may seem desperate to us, but it does not deter Jesus. Before this moment of divine intimacy between Father and Son, Jesus speaks of his mission to his friends. Now he speaks to his Father alone. Only once after this prayer of contemplative presence will he speak again to them. These will be his final intimate words before his death. After that he will seek the shelter of divine silence. He will be in ceaseless prayer to the Father, a prayer interrupted only by a few brief words, consisting of responses to his judges, short exhortations to his disciples, and invocations of his Father.

Though he is still present bodily among people, Jesus' heart already transcends in prayer the frontiers of humanity. He celebrates the Trinitarian life of self-emptying love. He expresses his prayer of divine transcendence in words so deep that they will be a source of inspiration for centuries to come.

We are called to share by grace in the same Trinitarian life that makes Jesus the eternal Son of God. All that is to happen to him, he takes up in advance within this prayer. He expresses his love in powerful words of worship and gratitude. Shortly hereafter he will express the same love with his blood. Then his captors will deprive him of all external dignity; now his prayer radiates the sublime dignity of a love freely given in self-surrender.

His prayer sounds as festive as the proclamation of the eucharist. At times it reaches the height of exultation. The words *glorify, glorified, glory* come up again and again. They set the tone, they provide the recurrent theme of joy that marks the last song of Jesus' heart on earth.

The Lord pours his whole being into these words of grateful praise. He thanks the Father for allowing him to sacrifice his life for a new creation that will enable us to share in the eternal Trinitarian life of love. He also consecrates us, by way of our participation in this prayer, to his divine life of sacrifice and compassionate service of others.

Loving Prayer

Loving prayer of the Lord,
Joyful words of adoration,
Saying thanks in an oblation
Of human life.
Song of love, of aspiration,
Consecrating everything
We say and do.

Loving prayer
Rising softly
From your likeness in the soul
Released into our longing heart,
Pervading life with sacrifice
And sweet surrender.

Loving prayer
Healing the self despisal
That unexpected failure
Breeds in excited minds,
Winding down
Into the chambers of anxiety
That imprison potencies for joy.

Loving prayer
Slaying foolish pride,
Poison of humanity, source of war,
Mother of cruelty and subtle slander,
Blight on the community of humankind.
O let your lovefilled prayer
Lift degraded life

To a festive chant of Eucharist
In the midst of persecution
By the Evil One.

1.

Dread of the Divine and Care for the Most Abandoned Souls

John 17:1

After saying this,
Jesus raised his eyes to heaven and said:
"Father, the hour has come."

Lord, you address God as "Father." This word of intimacy is hidden as a jewel in all your prayers. It does not stay concealed within your communication. No, it shines forth like a soft and steady light into your nights and days. Its meaning keeps your movements light-hearted, resilient, and graceful. You feel loved by the Father continuously, buoyed up and carried by his presence. You invite us gently to share in your life and its graced vitality. You ask us to become graceful, light-hearted, compassionate because God is our Father, too. You call us to radiate this compassion to others around us, especially those who are pained and downhearted.

Sometimes life wounds us and scares us. We feel lonely in crowds that seem to carry us along like leaves drifting aimlessly in a hurried stream. You gather us up like so many scattered leaves. You give us a life of meaning. Your life becomes our life with the Father.

To share your life is to share your convictions. The deepest conviction that refreshed and sustained you was always one and the same: God is Father. He loves us. He does what is best for us. He does not interfere with the free will of those who mistreat us. But he helps us to cope with evil and misunderstanding, to make the best of it. He enables us to sustain others in their suffering.

God is like a kind human father who helps his children to sustain the loss and adversity he cannot prevent from happening to them. He surrounds us with the best of care. He bends over our daily lives like a loving mother in care and confirmation.

Do I, as his child, really share your conviction of the Father's love? Do I share it when the hour of failure suddenly strikes? When depression creeps treacherously into my heart? Is God a Father for me? The exquisite One who brightens my days and frees my heart? Or do I secretly fear God? Is he for me a merciless judge? A resentful overseer? A taskmaster ready to pounce on the slightest mistake?

You came to free us from irrational guilt and fear, from the futile quest for perfectionism that comes in their wake. How prone we are to be fearful of God. Awe for his majesty, his dazzling purity, his mighty justice fills us with dread. You know better than we how dread of the Divine disturbed humanity over the ages. Religions of dread emerged from this anxiety. In some of them people were sacrificed to placate a God whom they did not know. They tore out human hearts, sacrificing them wantonly to temper the divine wrath. They imagined God's anger as a deadly cloud, as a somber sky hanging over humanity, ready to inflict destruction without measure.

You came to heal that festering wound. You taught people to pray to God as their Father. Did your message reach me, Jesus? Did it touch my heart, still my fear, calm the guilt that eats away at me? Or do these shadows of a primitive dread of the

Divine linger in my life even now? Do I temper this fear in people by showing them the love of Jesus?

This cancer poisons human life. It is like a disease at the heart of false religion and fictitious spirituality. Is this why your prayer to the Father had as its purpose to set me free every day a little more? Or does the old dread undermine my understanding that yours is a teaching of love? Do your words become one burden more to weigh me down?

We meet people who have cut themselves off from your teachings. They say with conviction that leaving religion behind was a relief. They never experienced God as a loving Father. They misinterpreted your message. Perhaps their parents were paralyzed by the anxiety of old that saw God only as a judge over them, not a Father who understands and forgives them, who gently affirms their hesitant attempts to grow in spiritual maturity. What else could they do but form their children in their own anxious image? The father in their family became the image not of a God of love but of a God of wrath. They suffered the worst kind of child abuse. This was not abuse of only the body, however terrible that is, but also abuse of the spirit. Their vulnerable spirit was poisoned. A false image of fatherhood began to shape their life. They heard you speak about God as Father. It did not evoke in them the image of a God of love. Your word reminded them of their own forbidding father or of others who played a domineering father-role in their lives. It spoiled your word for them. The hold of dread of the Divine resumed its power, so in panic they fled away from you.

Let all of us share, O Lord, in your awareness of the Father's love. Cure the dread of the Divine that hardens hearts and poisons minds. Heal the wounds of childhood that left so many souls—in the midst of material abundance—spiritually abandoned and alone. Especially touch the most poor and abandoned souls among them. Their inner poverty and misery may be camouflaged by a well-nourished body and an educated mind, by suburban homes and glittering cars. How much more abandoned they are than simple people here and abroad who believe in divine powers, no matter how little they are understood. How difficult it is to reach these most abandoned souls. How little do they reward those who come to them in your name. They withhold the gratitude and admiration simple people bestow so generously. How we, your disciples, fear their pride and arrogance, their sarcasm and skepticism, their learning, cynicism, and sophistication. How much we prefer the awe and sympathy others less educated may bestow on us. Without us even realizing it, they satisfy our need to feel needed.

Leaving these recalcitrant, most abandoned souls to their own devices, we may travel to distant lands to find less abandoned souls. Maybe they will comply more easily with our words. Maybe they will grant us the adoration we unwittingly desire.

Lord, while it is good and necessary to be an image of your Father for simple people, it is not enough to stop there. You want us to care for all people. Let the physical well-being and sophistication of others not prevent us from seeing their abandoned souls as well. Don't allow us to forget them, even though their cynicism may make us cringe. It was also for these spiritually poor that you gave your blood. May the fire of your love in us melt the wall of refusal that imprisons all wounded hearts wherever they may be.

Dread of the Divine

Dread of the Divine
That turns the heart
Into a mine
Of black despair.
How can we bear
With the wrath
That haunts our path
Like a vulture
Poised to pounce
On the race
That culture after culture
Wards off the raid
Of irate gods.
Dread of the Divine
Born in souls worn out
By abandonment and guilt.
The anger of the gods
Became the deadly cloud,
The somber sky
Hanging down oppressively
Over humanity in fear,
Threatening to rain
Hailstones of affliction.
Dread of the Divine,
Cancer that poisons
Human life,
Source of strife,
Burden that weighs down
Our flight to the stars.
. . . You came

As the defenseless babe
Of Bethlehem.
The lighthearted boy
Of Nazareth,
The gentle friend
Of abandoned souls
In Israel,
The sufferer
On a cross
To restore our loss
Of trust in God
As Father
Who does not hover
As a vulture over
Our dissolving life,
Who wants peace,
Not affliction, strife,
Who gathers us tenderly
As fallen leaves
From a dying tree
Miraculously
Restored to life.

2.

The Closure
of the Earthly Window

John 17:1

Father, the hour has come;
glorify your Son
so that your Son may glorify you.

Before this last supper, Jesus, you often said to your disciples: "My hour has not yet come." Now you say, "Father, the hour has come." Now is the time to celebrate the summit of your mission.

Your attunement to the Father makes you sense that *this is the sublime moment*. With courage you affirm the hour. You say yes to it. You accept that it is here, you flow silently with its mysterious message. The only thing that counts for you is conformity to the Father's will, for this is "the hour."

For us, too, that special hour, the finale of our life, will come. It is an hour we cannot escape, the hour of closure of our earthly window.

How we live that hour of sorrow and faith will give final form to our existence. All that went before it will be of no avail if we do not know how to surrender to life's final transition.

To be sure, our body will rebel as yours did in the garden. Deepen our faith, Lord Jesus, that in the end you will enable us to surrender, as you did, to the Father's desire in trust and love. Grant us the grace of attunement to the Father's will so that we, too, may sense that it is not cruel fate but eternal love that sets this final stage of our life.

Let us pray in and with you for brothers and sisters who are dying anywhere in the world. Let us share your passion on their behalf. Give them the final grace of salvation.

Your whole passage on earth can be seen as a prelude to this instant of wrenching yet redeeming closure. The hour loomed steadily before you. It was at the same time threatening in its absence and beckoning in its presence. Is that not why you said, "The hour has not yet come," while you also knew that it was near?

Grant us the wisdom to live in the light of our hour as it steadily approaches. Make our days like gentle waves ebbing and flowing in fluent harmony with the distant shores that await us. Every day many are summoned to face that night. Assist them, Jesus, in their agony. Touch them with the sweet confidence of your surrender to the Eternal. Make the final hour their finest, no matter what went before it. Your compassion heals wounds, softens pain, relieves fear, forgives sins, if we only trust in you.

To be mindful of our hour makes us less inclined to lose ourselves in empty pursuits of earthly glory. The hunt for human esteem makes it difficult to seek and find the Father's will at the decisive moments of our pilgrimage.

The pride that permeates our fallen life causes us to forget your image and likeness in the inmost depths of our being. The more we allow willfulness to dominate our life, the more it will weigh us down at the decisive time that we receive the Father's invitation to share in your ascent to glory.

Preparing for this hour and its agony you pray: "Glorify your Son so that your Son may glorify you." These words highlight the profound meaning this hour had for you. Its deepest sense resides in the one word you repeat again and again, the word "glory." Glory is proper to God. Glory lets God appear as God. Glory is the manifestation of the splendor of God's being.

Only God can be glorified as ultimate goodness, truth, and beauty. Only God can let his glory shine forth in all created things. This light divine manifests itself above all in your sacred humanity. So you pray: "Glorify your Son."

You ask your Father for a paradoxical favor, namely, that his glory may manifest itself in the hour of your own defeat and death. This is your way of saying: "I surrender to your will, Father. I do not ask for human glory; only your glory counts for me. I may look like a fool in the eyes of people. Many may see me as an abysmal failure. They may scorn me as a dreamer who lived in vain for a fleeting mirage that could never come true. They scoff at me as a lowly carpenter of Nazareth, who ends his life as a 'Messiah'—as nothing but a criminal hanging on a cross between thieves. Father, I accept this sacrifice of all worldly honor, this cancellation of any esteem. May your glory alone radiate in my failed life and broken body."

You pray that this divine glorification may fulfill every human hope. You pray earnestly for this favor, because you know it is impossible, humanly speaking, to bear with such debasement.

For you to be glorified in this hour implies the wanton destruction of anything in your appearance that could evoke esteem in worldly people. Only when you are the Crucified One can you enter into the true splendor of the Father's plan for your life. Remember, it was you who said: "The Messiah must suffer and so enter into his glory." You knew that obedience and humility open human nature to divine glorification. That is why you anticipated glory in the debasement that awaited you.

And so you pray: "Glorify your Son so that your Son may glorify you." The Father turns your defeat into glory as you aspire to manifest the power and splendor of the Father. You do so by showing us that surrender to the Father in obedience carries with it the sting of suffering and death. You praise the Father by your fidelity to all that he asks you to endure for our sake. When you leave this vale of tears, you will glorify the Father everlastingly. When the Father has raised you up, you will not rest only in the gift of your own glorified humanity. You want the Father to be praised by countless others who share in your glorification.

By the power of your Spirit you seek to transform our lives. Through us you want to be present as a transforming power in history for all people. So you embrace the desperate multitudes who populate the earth as it rotates slowly to its end. You make this mere speck of dust in the unfathomable cosmos a place of epiphanic disclosure of your compassion for us, with us, through us.

Thérèse of Lisieux tells us that she does not imagine her heaven to be a place of enjoyment only. She asks God to make of her heaven a lasting opportunity to do good to people on earth. Her vision is in tune with your Spirit and with the message of your testament. To be glorified ourselves is not the highest goal we can reach. The highest meaning of life is to glorify God, to be a perpetual flame symbolizing devotion to his name. Help us to make your Father's glory known everywhere. Create in us clean hearts with plenty of room for self-emptying compassion for others.

If you had prayed only, "Glorify your Son," your prayer could have connoted narrowness of vision. It might have obscured for us the scope of your mission. But when you added, "so that your Son may glorify you," everything fell into perspective.

With these words you revealed to us that God incarnated the glory of his divine, eternal life in your humanity. Your glorified nature thus becomes the model of our Christian life, the well-spring of our transformation, the pathway through suffering into glory. You are for us the focal point of the universe. In you the loving, transforming power of God pours itself out limitlessly. You heal a humanity sinful and unfree, out of touch with the divinization we were created to enjoy eternally.

Gentle Closure

You gently close
The window of this life,
You end its strife,
Bringing our ship
Into your port,
Displacing our worry
With your glory,
Dispelling what is base
By the glory of your face.

Make us repent
The ways we went
Astray, away from home
To build the dome
Of human glory,
To tell the story
Of things achieved
Leaving you alone
To grieve.

Make our days
Like gentle waves
That rise and fall in harmony
With the music of eternity
Until the secret rhyme
Of our lives in time
Stands revealed.
Embrace, O Lord
The multitudes

That populate this planet
Rotating slowly
Like a speck of dust
Amidst the silence
Of the stars.

3.

Consonance
with the Trinity

John 17:2

Just as you have given him
power over all humanity
he may give eternal life to all those
you have entrusted to him.

While preparing for your passion and death, you are already aware of the power of grace and salvation that will be yours that Easter day. At this moment your heart goes out not only to your Father but to all people. Because of your redeeming death, all humanity will be overshadowed by your canopy of care. Your heart embraces each person who ever walked on the earth. You delight that it will be in your power to give them eternal life.

Your Father formed humanity in the divine image. Each person was called to express that image uniquely in his or her life. Since the Fall it has become difficult for us to keep in tune with this form of God in our soul.

How painfully you knew that our daily life was no longer animated by the image of your Father. We became empty, more dissonant than consonant, pedestrian and narrow-minded. We lost the will to keep in touch with our eternal Source.

Now, despite our sin, you restore our potency to participate in the life of God imaged in our own soul. Through the gift of your redemption, people are once again able to mirror the image of your self-emptying love in their inmost being and in every human relationship.

Your life permeates our daily growth giving it the radiance of eternity. Following you not only restores us to our divine image; it elevates us to a sharing in the mystery of self-giving love that is at the heart of the Holy Trinity.

In you, Son of God and Eternal Word, we participate as "little words." Through your infinite generosity, you make us share in the community of the Trinity.

Help us, Jesus, not to live in forgetfulness of the miracle of love that has happened to us without our deserving it. Grant us the gift of formative memory so that we may live in remembrance of your mysterious presence in and among us.

You tell us, Jesus, what this "giving of eternal life" really means. It is a knowing of your Father as the only true God. This miraculous knowledge also implies a knowing of you as being sent by, as going forth from, the Father.

The kind of knowing you offer to give your disciples is not simply a conveying of information. This knowledge affects our spiritual formation. It sheds light on God's presence while concealing his essence. The Godhead is far beyond anything we can conceive or imagine, yet in you the transcendent becomes immanent. The knowledge you give lets us share wholeheartedly in the mystery of divinity. Only you can grant us heart knowledge in love and surrender. It at once satiates and increases our restless desire for oneness with you.

This precious knowledge grants us an abundance of peace and joy. It presupposes that we are so grasped by the depth and beauty of the divine that our whole existence benefits from the grace of a true conversion. That is why, Jesus, the formative knowledge of God, granted to us by you, truly transforms our life.

You add that eternal life is also a knowing of you as the Christ sent by the Father to be our savior. You assure us that we are called to enter into a living, transforming knowledge of the God who made himself known to us in you, his only begotten Son. You try in word and deed to make us aware that our destiny is to share in the eternal life of the Trinity in and through you, the Christ form of our soul.

The Father knows himself in you as his eternal, divine image. The Son knows himself in the Father. For you say that everything has been entrusted to you by your Father. No one knows the Son except the Father, just as no one knows the Father except the Son and those to whom the Son chooses to reveal him (Mt 11:27).

Before the revelation, we did not know anything about the inner life of God. Not knowing meant that we could not participate by faith in the life of the most Holy Trinity. Now, in this love song of yours, everything changes. You ask the Father to grant us a share in this divine community, a sharing that happens in the darkness of faith. It is a believing while knowing and a knowing while believing. This knowledge of the heart gradually transforms the way in which we express our divinization in daily living. We discover day by day the presence of the Trinity

in ourselves and in every person we encounter in
your name. Help us to image the divine life of
Father, Son, and Holy Spirit in the love we show to
one another.

Epiphany of Divinity

Shalom is your legacy,
Consonance of mind
For those you left behind
To die in ignomy.
Your broken body
Is an epiphany of serenity
For suffering humanity.
The sun breaks gloriously
From behind the clouds
Drenching us in light.
So is the might
Of each beam of mercy
Piercing our night,
Gushing from a gaping wound
Around each rusty nail.
To be an epiphany of divinity
Is the destiny
Of redeemed humanity.
Transfigured are
Lakes and mountains,
Fresh, resplendent
Flowers, woods, and fountains,
Pristine beauty
Clothes the meadow.
Everything is soft and mellow,
Everything is new again
Because the Lord is slain.

4.

Eternal Exit
from the Cage of Time

John 17:3

And eternal life is this:
to know you, the only true God,
and Jesus Christ whom you have sent.

Your hour has come, Beloved. Unforgettable is your prayer for us at this crucial moment. Awaiting you is sorrow, suffering, death. Yet it does not occur to you to ask the Father to spare you from this pending torture. You beg him to let you bear the coming affliction in a spirit of grateful surrender that shall glorify his name. Then you ask that through your passion eternal life may be granted to those souls entrusted to your care.

Your prayer lights up the meaning of this gift of utter self-donation. The promise of eternal life transforms our understanding. It is not merely an intellectual grasping but a knowing of the heart that involves our whole being. We receive from you the gift of living in the presence to the Holy. You, Lord Jesus, have been sent to save us from our sins. You are the epiphany of the infinite mystery embracing creation and silently penetrating its history.

At times you spoke of this life of presence as something that is already ours here and now. At other times you revealed it as something awaiting us in the hereafter. Both are true revelations. We are called to live this holy presence on earth, yet our awareness of its splendor will be limited until we exit the cage of time and enter the full light of eternity.

The peace of dwelling with the Eternal, for whom we long, is often disrupted by the cares of this age. Yet thanks to your grace, we can return to the still place within us. You dwell in our inmost center as a living presence to the Father. Our communion with you in an eternal face to face draws us into communion with others. You call us to oneness with the Trinity in the depths of our being and to loving care for our brothers and sisters in Christ. You make your home in us and among us. You are the source of our loving participation in a transcendent reality at once beyond us and within us.

Christian life flows from our response to your call uniquely and communally. In your light we strive to emulate divine generosity, patience, love, and humility. Our very trying leads us to a new set of life directives. Under the inspiration of your Spirit, we strive to appraise them wisely and gratefully. We accept what they inspire, and we allow these inspirations to form our life in a new fashion.

Your presence among us helps us to see the ways in which the eternal permeates time. The more your grace enables us to make your way our way, the more our life alone and together radiates a peace and joy the world in its worldliness cannot give. Our life begins to image in time the eternal life of the Trinity.

No longer do we drift along anxiously and aimlessly. No longer is our life restricted to the pursuit of functional ambitions or to the fulfillment of only vital needs. No longer is there "no exit" for us from the cage of time in which our life seems to peter out meaninglessly.

Thanks to your presence in and around us, daily duties involving our care for others receive a divine significance. Failures and disappointments, even suffering and dying, all have an eternal meaning. You bestow light and love on our lost and forlorn days. The winters of life, those dreary periods of forgetfulness of the transcendent, are fewer and farther between. You lift us again and again beyond our self-protective safety zones into the fresh spring of freely offered self-surrender. A feeling of peace overtakes us as your light floods through clouded windows of worry. We experience your priestly prayer as a silent invitation to become more like you every day in our love for others.

Such moments of illumination slowly fashion the slender thread of our life direction. No longer bound to petty endeavors, we allow the divine Weaver to refashion us in and through the pattern of our earthly existence. We sense the unfolding movement of our divine life call in every individual and communal endeavor.

What if we fail to enkindle the fire of eternity that wants to shine forth in our everyday presence and participation? Following the ways of the world, we may be commended for the efficiency of our performance, rewarded for a job well done, granted a promotion, but our accomplishments seem shallow. No longer are they an inspiration to our fellow pilgrims. We need to correct our course. Only when your eternal life enwraps our temporal existence can we find our way through the tempests of everydayness and answer the demands of those we serve in your name.

If we are in touch in time with the flow of eternity, we may be able to take in stride the tide of events and situations bombarding our shores. We begin to see life's ups and downs as the changing landscapes surrounding our journey. They are the challenges you put before us in compassionate love. Your mystery within us and among us is the precious compass that guides our frail ship through the churning waters of history.

A life of taking rather than giving veils the treasure within. That is why you invite us in your prayer song to pull away from ports of human security and to sail out into the vast ocean of your mystery of self-emptying in love. Give us the grace to trust that you will keep us afloat, no matter the ferocity of any storm.

You tell us, Lord Jesus, that our eternal life is not only to know the true God, but to know you yourself whom he has sent. Only through your revelation can we lift a little the veil concealing the mystery of divinity. To know you means to receive the grace of intimacy with the Trinity and to witness the outpouring of God's love in the people around us. We begin to know you and the Father and the Holy Spirit in a new way. For what you call "knowing God" is like no other way of knowing. This revealed knowledge illumines our heart, evokes our compassion for suffering humanity, and grants us a new way of seeing the ways of God with us. This knowledge is mystical. By it we are grasped so totally by the truth of God's being that our whole life is suffused with this loving awareness.

You want to teach us about this way of knowing. It is less intellectualistic and more experiential, less piecemeal and more comprehensive, less deadening and more alive. Ultimately you want us to know about the Father's loving presence to you and yours. You assure us by your prayer that we are called to share in the Trinitarian mystery of self-emptying love. You tell us to rejoice in the Father, who has made himself known in you, his eternal Son. You reveal to us that he knows himself in the Son and the Son in the Father.

> Everything has been entrusted to me by my Father; and no one knows the Son except the Father, just as no one knows the Father except the Son and those to whom the Son chooses to reveal him. (Mt 11:27)

As we come to know God in the splendor of this Trinitarian life of love, we begin to know how to live as an adoptive child of the Trinity in daily life. Our relationship with Father, Son, and Holy Spirit happens not only in our interiority; it also starts to transform our interpersonal relationships. Through our knowing in faith and our living in love the life of the Trinity, we share the gift of your saving hope for us.

Lord Jesus, you reveal the fullness of faith, hope, and love in your priestly prayer. That is why we pray that you will make ours, too, a living faith, an undying hope, a self-giving love. Let us share more and more in the mystery of your own presence to the Father in the Holy Spirit. Show us how to celebrate this presence in the depths of our being while we care daily for others. Allow the light of eternity to shine forth in every human encounter, in every temporal endeavor, as we model for one another the beauty, truth, and goodness of Trinitarian love.

Epiphany of Mystery

Epiphany of Mystery
Silently embracing
Emergence of creation,
Transforming humanity
By gracious pervasion.
Mystery of gentle grace,
Illumine our ways,
Disclose the eternal exit
From the cage of time,
The empty, trying days,
A caravan of tired camels.
Eternal spark within
Pierce the dreary winter
Of forgetfulness of the Divine.
Clean the clouded window,
Weave threads of light
Through our nights.
Make us risk
The mysterious voyage
Of light and love.
Lighthouse, guide
Our little ships
Tossing on the churning
Waters of history.
Keep afloat the battered boats

Of fleeting lives.
Make us celebrate
Your presence in the depths
Of our being.

5.

A Song of the Name
at the End of Jesus' Journey

John 17:4

*I have glorified you on earth
by finishing the work
that you gave me to do.*

Approaching the end of your life, you look back on it gently, Lord Jesus. The whole of it passes before your eyes. It was a good life, as we want ours to be. What else is life than a task to be fulfilled, a divine assignment to undertake, an expression of trust, in our short, perilous journey through time and space? Think of how quickly your journey ended. It lasted for only thirty-three years. What mattered was not the length of your life but its loving integrity.

Your life was a song of gentle, yet firm fidelity to what the Father asked of you. Grant us too the grace of being faithful to our destiny in his name.

The overall meaning of our life cannot be reduced to any one episode of success or failure. We perform so many chores from day to day: doing the laundry, cleaning the dishes, dressing the children, writing a paper, building a house, caring for the needy. To be sure, these works are also the Father's will for us. You bless us when we try to do them with the same joy and love with which you did your daily chores in Nazareth. Even these small achievements have something to do with the life's work the Father meant for us from eternity.

Your own hidden life is our inspiration. We call to mind your play with other children, your learning of the Hebrew scriptures, your carpentry with St. Joseph for the people of Nazareth, your obedient service to Mary around the house. Each detail had something to do with the destiny the Father had called you to fulfill.

Yet none of these events in and by themselves could explain the fullness of the revelation that made your life truly yours.

As your priestly prayer unfolds, you tell us what your life's task really was: "I have revealed your name to those whom you took from the world to give me" (Jn 17:6).

Is it our task to share in some way in this task of yours to make known the Father's name? What would doing so mean? What is the Father's name? In holy scripture a name is not simply an external label attached to a person like an identification card or a sign along the road. The name expresses the unique mystery of a person. In the case of an eminent personality, it represents something about him or her that remains etched in our memory.

Making the name of the Father known means letting his beauty, truth, and goodness shine through us to others. You did just that in ways we cannot equal: in the suffering and death awaiting you after this last supper and, most eminently, in your glorious resurrection.

Your life in Nazareth was also a song of his name. The brightness of the Father's glory shone forth in your smile, in the flow of your movements when you served at table, ran joyfully with the other children in the market place, carried the water jar for Mary, or drove nails into the polished wood of a table or chair you and Joseph were making for a neighbor in need.

The silent music of your movements gave eloquent voice to the name of your heavenly Father. Our life, too, must be a reflection of continual reverence for the name. Otherwise we might live it in vain. How empty our life would be were it not a sharing in your eternal song to the graciousness and glory of God. You ask us to seek and find the Father's will for us into the succession of situations that link our life together. They are like a string of pearls woven one by one by a loving hand.

Some of these situations may bring us, as they did you, into the public arena, but here we must be careful. Pride may tempt us to boast of our own name more than to let the name of God come first. How grateful we are, Lord Jesus, when you spare us from that temptation. It is better to be called to imitate your inconspicuous life of Nazareth.

Most of us are chosen to bring the name of the Lord to others not in neon letters but in the scribbles of a child; not in splendid oratory, but in simple words of kindness and consolation; not in heroic deeds of peace and justice that capture headlines, but in quiet fidelity to neighbors and companions. While we may see our names in lights once in a while, we are happiest when we can enkindle a little candle of love in some small corner of our neighborhood or working place.

What matters is that in all that we are or do we glorify the Father's name on earth, that in and with and through you we finish the task he entrusted to us.

If only we could say as you did at the end of our life: "I have glorified you on earth and finished the work that you gave me to do." None of us will ever do so perfectly. All of us fail to live up to the fullness of this heavenly mission. Yet we still dare to make this promise, for you will fulfill it in us and for us. If we turn to you wholeheartedly in faith, hope, and love, at the final moment of our transition, you will never turn us away.

You spread the warm light of peace and mercy throughout the dying frame of our earthly existence. You forgive us. Then you complete what we did not do as we should have done for you and others around us. In our suffering body you sing to the eternal Father: "In this poor sinner, I have glorified you on earth. My glorified humanity perfects at once before you, Father, the work you gave this person to do. Please Father, for my sake, take this repentant soul into your eternal embrace of tender love. Remember, Father, that this soul, too, is one of those you gave to me from the world."

A Song of Everlasting Praise

Let me sing a song to your name
When I leave my frame
At the end of my perilous journey.
Let my tearful eyes look back
In sorrow at the dusty tracks
Of a life that failed so often
To fulfill the task you assigned to me.
Forgive my lack of fidelity
To the candle I was to be,
To keep alight your mystery
In a small corner of this earth.
Remind me of my destiny:
To let eternal life shine forth a little
In my own pedestrian way
Joyfully from day to day
Until the journey ends
And boundless light begins.
Let the brightness of your glory
Sing in the music of movement,
In words of joy and animation.
A sharing in the song of praise
That is your risen life.
Show me in the light of faith,
The procession of my life's events
As a chain of pearls

Woven tenderly by an eternal hand.
And when my journey ends,
Sing for me to Father
Your dying song of everlasting praise
That makes my life complete
Despite its countless failures.

6.

Before the World Ever Was

John 17:5

Now, Father,
glorify me with that glory I had
with you before ever the world existed.

O Jesus, we adore the mystery of your intimacy with the Father, a mystery in which we share minute by minute. A love beyond imagining illumines our life, making the shadows of everydayness sparkle with meaning. It makes us touch the lives of others with the brightness of heartfelt care.

Your glory was hidden from human eyes for most of your life. But now, at this last supper, the moment is near when the veil of time will be lifted. Then will the glory of eternity explode in the battered frame of your bruised face and broken body. For our sake you hide your might and majesty. You relinquish freely and joyfully the glory that was yours before the world began.

Now at this last gathering with your disciples, you know that the depletion of your infinite dignity will soon reach its awesome depth. Debasement awaits you, stripping, scourging, and being crowned with thorns. But after your shameful death your humanity will rise to enduring glory. The glory that already is yours as the eternal word of God will shine forth unabated in your humanity.

We adore the boundless generosity of your divine love for our fallen race. What honor you brought to the earth! You made this puny needlepoint, whirling slowly in an immense universe, your dwelling place. You humbly descended on this pellet dwarfed by giant suns and vast constellations. You became an inhabitant on this tiny speck of dust, investing it with the full glory of its Creator. It is not an angel who will be enthroned in divine resplendence but a human being with a body, mind, will, and heart, with eyes, hands and feet, whose gaping wounds will be an epiphany of the mystery of self-emptying love. Angels and archangels will prostrate themselves in adoration of your divinity and your humanity.

Why has our race been singled out by the Father for such lasting glory? Our voice falters because there is no adequate reply. Our mind is stunned; our heart is overcome by such love. What honor you brought to this strange and sinful people! What love now invades lonely planet earth.

We are left speechless with wonder that your glorified humanity will take our humanity up and transform it. Our humanness with all its imperfection will reflect your resurrected glory. Just as a clear mountain lake mirrors the beauty of the sun above it, so will our redeemed humanity be radiant with your beauty. The Father will delight in the way your splendor lights up in us, for you have both honored him and saved us by your blood.

"God, our Father, glorious in giving life and even more glorious in restoring it; when his last night on earth came, your Son shed tears of blood, but brought down incomparable gladness. Do not turn away from us, or we shall fall back into dust, but rather turn our mourning into joy by raising us up with Christ" (Holy Office, Ordinary Time, Week 1).

Rising up in Christ, sharing his glory, is our destiny in time and eternity. That glory was yours, Jesus Lord, before the world came to be. In some way it was ours also, for all of us share your life. Before we came to be in time, we existed in eternity in the Father's vision of creation. Our face and form were in his sight before we were born. The unique form loved by him before all ages would unfold in our life as we imaged him in time and space.

Awesome as it is to say, we have been preformed in the bosom of the Trinity, cradled in the gentle design of God from the beginning, even before the universe exploded in terrifying splendor. The creation of our unique form of life was like a word spoken out eternally by the Father in his divine Word in whom everything came to be.

In you, eternal Word, we can find back in faith the form of life meant for us from eternity. In you, too, rests the mystery of the face that was ours, our essence, before we came into existence. That face constitutes our deepest identity, our highest "I." Help us by your grace to radiate the glory of God in our life and the lives of all those in need of our care.

Alas, we must admit in sorrow that the original form of glory intended for us by you did not reach full unfolding in any of us. The fall of humanity veiled and deformed our founding life form made in the image and likeness of God, but it did not take away all possibility of conformity to Christ. Through his death and resurrection, you made possible our redemption and return to you.

All people of good will remain in search of a lost paradise of spoiled love and glory. What is that secret stone with our true name inscribed on it? That holy grail? That pearl of great price? These images point to the forgotten treasure of our inmost face, of our glorious original form in you that, through baptism, becomes the Christ form of our soul.

We feel the need for reformation of our scarred and misdirected lives. In some measure the marvel of divine transformation can restore us to our original splendor. Ignatius of Antioch exhorts us to "look for him who is outside time, the eternal one, the unseen, who became visible for us; he cannot be touched and cannot suffer, yet he became subject to suffering and endured so much for our sake."

Inserting yourself, divine Word, into our human nature, you transformed it, so to say, from the inside out. You saved us by your blood from the sin that cripples the forming power of grace in our soul. It mars the potential glorified splendor of a heart in love with you. It makes us miss the mark.

Despite sin, you give us the grace of repentance, and you infuse us with your glory. You transform us into participants in the eternal life and love of the Trinity. You enable us to radiate this love in and with Jesus to all people we meet.

Assume us, O Lord, into your holy humanity. Make us share in your own glory, the glory that was yours before the world began. Then will our face and form, in radiant transformation, reveal your face and form to everyone around us. Then will the Father delight eternally in seeing the face of his Son, the Christ form of our soul, shining forth epiphanically in our earthly existence.

The Face that Was Mine

Before the world ever was
The song of birds, the green of grass,
The sun, the moon, the dance of stars,
The rivers, streams, the spruce and spars,
Before we were in woe and worry
There was the marvel of your glory.
We twinkled in its loving light,
Like little jewels in the bright
Prevision of what was to be
In time and in eternity.
O, the face that was mine
Before emerging in time.
The purity of form
That should be the norm
Of my unfolding life
Before anxious strife
Deformed my eternal beauty.
I refused the duty
Of forming life in your image Lord.
Yet, embraced by your Word,
I found the providential worth of everything
In life. The Word became the wing
That drew me gently home,
No longer lost, alone.
The Word became my transformation
In the marvel of your incarnation,
Revealing the form meant for me,
That flows from you, shall ever be.

7.

The Name of the Recklessly Tender One

John 17:6

I have revealed your name
to those whom you took from the world
to give me.

John 17:11

Holy Father,
keep those you have given me true to your
name so that they may be one like us.

The beginning of the second part of your testament is like a melody of love that reverberates in our inmost being. How infinitely you care for the likes of us! The Father has entrusted us to your love, and we know you will not leave us orphaned.

You pray that our lives will be transformed into his resplendent image. We are given to you out of the world to resist, with your help, its image of success. The world with its prideful pulsations threatens to seduce us. Exaltation, autonomy, cults of self-assertion remind us that the world is too much with us. No wonder you pray explicitly for the people of faith given to you by the Father. You want us to pray and work for them, as you did, with compassion and forgiveness.

In the first part of your prayer you do not ask for yourself alone, for your own glory, but for the glory that already embraces us, too. First you ask the Father to give glory to your human life here with us. This glory is the consummation of your mission to our race. Fidelity to your eternal call means that you will make the Father's love wholly present to all people. You keep nothing for yourself alone. Rather, the formation of your humanity into everlasting glory makes possible the transformation of the people who share in the light and grace of your divine life.

Such truths cannot be told all at once. Sharing our human nature means that you share in its limitations of thinking and speaking. Like us, you cannot express all that you mean in one sentence only. You can only make clear gradually what the glory you ask for means to each of us and to all of us entrusted to your care. You want us to become aware of what the glorious form of your humanity holds in store for your apostles and for us, your disciples. Then you let us see how we are called in turn to be the graced carriers of your presence, the joyful mediators of your message, in the world.

With love and reverence you speak to us about the "name of God." "I have revealed your name. . . . Holy Father, keep those you gave me true to your name." In the name you want us to know something of God's essence, of the mystery of divinity that can never be disclosed totally.

The art of naming is age-old. Tribal peoples, who live together for a long time in the intimacy of a community, are often able to express in one striking name the essential core of each other's personality.

Similarly, people in love often use endearing names for one another. They express some quality only love can see in the beloved. It is a name only they may know. It is kept secretly between them because it reveals something of their private life. Even if the name were spoken publicly, others would not be able to penetrate its full meaning. They have no way of sharing in the history of love between the people so named in this fashion.

Something similar happens in the enchanting love story between God, the Father, and the people he formed in love. In infinite generosity your Father unveiled to the sons and daughters of Abraham, Isaac, and Jacob the name by which he would be called, Yahweh or "I am who am." What was surprising was not only the name itself but the fact that God allowed the people to call him by name.

At that period of history people felt as if they had power over those whose name they could master, as if it contained the secret of their strength. They assumed that the all-mighty divinity would remain unspeakable, that he could never be named. How startled they were that your Father allowed them to call him by the name he himself revealed to them. To the chosen people this revelation was an awesome demonstration of your Father's trust. And yet we learn from your prayer that this gift of the divine name to the Hebrews was only the beginning of your Father's self-unveiling.

Your call, Lord, was to bring the Father near to us. You yourself would be named Emmanuel, "God with us." The forming presence of the divinity as Holy Trinity would be made more intimately known to us by you, the only-begotten Son of God, who took on our wounded flesh.

"I have revealed your name." You opened for people a whole new path to the heart of Divinity. The revelation you gave us about God's being is made clear both in what you say and in who you are. That is why your every word has about it an inexhaustible depth.

The word "Father" had been applied to God long before your appearance on earth. But nowhere could this familiar word gain the full significance you granted it by your own living of the name and your exemplary address to God as "Abba," or "Daddy."

Your incarnation was a blessing greater than any we could have expected in our boldest dreams. It meant, among other things, that you had to express yourself in words familiar to us, words like "Abba." What you unveil by means of common parlance is infinitely original. It represents a divine self-communication we are privileged to hear. It gives us a glimpse of the splendor of eternal light.

You transform the power of language as you transform the people who hear your word. Your "Father" is unlike any earthly father. He is love. In telling us of "Abba," you opened up a whole new world for us. You did so by revealing that you are the Son, who in his very being is like the Father. You let us see in your humanity that God loved the world in a way none of us could have imagined or deserved. By your life you make the Fatherhood of God transparent to humanity.

All too often our human experience of fatherhood is distorted. Many earthly fathers fail their calling. They lack fidelity to the kind of formative parenting for which they are responsible. Many succumb to other desires and desert spouses and mothers. Even the best of fathers is limited in his amount of generosity, patience, and compassion. It is hard for any human father to express fully the loving presence of your Father to our daily needs. All human fathers need your help to become warm and loving expressions of your divine fatherhood. That is why only Jesus could say: "Who sees me sees the Father."

To be loved by you is to be lifted beyond the history of our personally formative or deformative fatherexperience. Your presence purifies our past and our future from pain and limitation. When we allow you to say in our heart, "Abba Father," it is as if heaven itself opens its door. Thus you taught us to say, "Our Father, who art in heaven." You asked us to reverence his name because it points to the inexpressible mystery of a fatherhood that transcends any human category. Hence we pray, "Hallowed be your name."

Your Father's love is so all-encompassing, so sweet and gentle, that it also contains the tenderness symbolized by motherhood. God is our heavenly father, our nurturing mother, qualities manifested beautifully in your life, Lord Jesus.

Thank you, most tender Son, for making the Father familiar to us in you. Nobody can know the Father without you. Forgive us for ever imagining we can know him while neglecting to abide with you.

We may acknowledge him reverently as Creator, as Judge, as the Almighty. But these ancient forms in which God appears are too limited, too one-sided. They do not temper our hidden fear, our secret trembling. They imply that God may only be anxiety-evoking, punishing, terrifying, incomprehensible. Many became non-believers to escape the dread of the Divine that paralyzes their life. It can be awful to face the Almighty without the softening prism of your human reflection of the Godhead.

Some may claim it is easier to meet God in nature than in the Church or the scriptures. Yet nature is only an incomplete manifestation of the Infinite. It can be as enchanting as a spring evening, as noble as a peacock, as sublime as a snowy peak. But nature can also be as merciless as a tornado, as cruel as a hungry vulture, as catastrophic as an avalanche.

Without you, Lord Jesus, there is a dizzying distance between the Father and us. Nothing can bridge the abyss that separates us: He is all powerful, we powerless; he is saintliness, we are sin; he is purity, we are corruption; he is wisdom infinite, we are small-mindedness; he is just and generous; we are dishonest, mean and greedy. There is no bridge, no exit from our mean condition, no entrance into the ˙ ·stery of the Father's generosity without your sacred humanity. You alone can lead us to appreciate the deepest meaning of the name of the recklessly tender One, the lovely name of "Abba."

A Melody of Tender Love

A melody of tender love
Sings in my inmost being,
The sweet and snowy dove
Of love dwells in my deepest feeling.
The splendor of the living Lord
Lights up the Father's name.
When lived by the eternal Word.
This word is not the same
As it was known before
In common word and speech.
It was only a symbol, a metaphor
Of love beyond my reach.
Then you descended in my life,
O mediator of the name.
You kindled in my weary heart
The everlasting flame
Dancing between you and him,
Lifting me beyond my power,
Pushing me beyond the rim
Of any mental tower
Of wisdom, strength, and might
Built by human sight,
Clever, straight and right
And yet not wrought
By you alone, my God.

Thank you for this sweet unveiling
Of what is beyond human tongue.
Let us not be failing
The Father for whom we long,
For whom we pine so desperately,
The Father we lose unknowingly
When we misdirect our search for you
To failing fathers here on earth.

8.

Gifts of Unspeakable Grace

John 17:6

*"They were yours
and you gave them to me."*

Lord, you give us yet another glimpse of the intimacy and mystery that radiate from the life of the Trinity: "They were yours. . ." What joy it gives us to hear in your words this assurance of who we truly are. You remind us that the Father loved us from all eternity and willed to save us because "They were yours. . ."

The past tense (*were*) does not imply that we are no longer the Father's treasured children, created tenderly in his image and likeness. We were, we are, we will always be his own. Now you tell us that the Father empowers us, through your holy humanity, to be in a new way his children.

We were already yours before your incarnation, suffering, and death. As the divine Word of the Father, you are the expression of his fullness. You hold within you from eternity all that exists and pre-exists in his caring, creative, and confirming love. We are, therefore, also held in you, his eternal Word.

Before all ages, before the explosive formation in time of the universe as we know it, despite our feeling of being dwarfed in space, you call us to a personal relationship with the source of all grace, the most Holy Trinity. You made us your own, and so we are infinitely more than this material universe.

The Father called us from eternity into Eternity. Though we lost this privilege of an everlasting joyful presence before his face, though sin crippled our flight, in his faithful love he sent you to transform our lives, to end our awful plight. He gave us to you so that you could present us to him once again unblemished due to your transfiguring presence in us and in all people open to your call.

The Father has handed us over to your care, Lord Jesus. You are the incarnated mystery of love that surrounds and sustains suffering humanity. We have been given to you so that you can return us, together in community, to the Father as a new creation. The way to his heart is through you, for you are the way:

> . . . and they have kept your word. Now at last they have recognized that all you have given me comes from you; for I have given them the teaching you gave to me, and they have indeed accepted it, and know for certain that I came from you, and have believed that it was you who sent me. (Jn 17:6-8)

The Father gave us to you, Word made flesh, divine mystery of human transformation. Our Creator made us free to consent or to refuse to be the Father's gift to you. We have it within us to reject this gift, to resist your loving power of transformation. Yet you came to set us free from sin, free to say yes to the divine created and uncreated powers of transformation emanating from the Trinity. Their mystical tide sweeps invisibly through space and time, through universe, world, humanity, and history. They surround, embrace, and penetrate all that is and will be.

These divine powers find their highest expression in the Father's enfleshed, eternal Word. Their mysterious intensity, their transforming energy, empowers your words, for they embody the wisdom of the Father for all ages. You ask us to open our hearts to these words of power, to cherish and keep them, to dwell on them without ceasing. We are to be witnesses to your words in the world, sources of light in a world darkened by sin. Others are to know us by the love we have for one another.

To keep your word is to be transfigured inwardly and outwardly. Your word is the bridge between us and others. It puts us in touch with the divine created and uncreated energies always at work in history. Just as a radio signal sometimes fades, so, too, do we tend to lose touch with your all pervading presence.

Through the power of the Spirit, help us to overcome our dissonance. Make us consonant with your word at every moment, one in spirit with the redeemed community of humanity. Teach us to keep your word as Mary did in her heart, to ponder and treasure its enlightening power.

Lord Jesus, through your grace let us taste and see the wisdom of the word. Help us to grasp experientially in faith that you are the eternal Word, co-equal with the Father, that the Father from eternity pours out in you the fullness of his divinity.

The Father and you are one, O Lord. You call us, unworthy though we are, to be one with you as you

and the Father are one. In faith, we accept your gift
of love. In trust, we adore your divinity and its
forming mystery in our lives. With hearts on fire
with love and hope, we hear you say:

> It is for them that I pray.
> I am not praying for the world
> but for those you have given me,
> because they belong to you.
> All I have is yours
> and all you have is mine,
> and in them I am glorified.
> I am no longer in the world,
> but they are in the world,
> and I am coming to you. . .
> I kept those you had given me true to your name.
> I have watched over them and not one is lost
> except the one who was destined to be lost,
> and this was to fulfill the scriptures. (Jn 17:9-12)

You offer this prayer for each of us. It is so
encouraging to know that you are "not praying for
the world but for those you have given me." You
make us feel so grateful. How can it be that we have
been chosen to be your own people? To be God's
gift to you? You return us to the Father. You allow
us to share in your own eternal, Trinitarian relationship of love, the love that is the essence of the divine
unity. You tell us in your prayer that you will be
glorified in your friends in time and eternity.

How moving it is to see how loyal you were to them at that Last Supper table. You loved them even while sensing their weakness. You knew that one of them would betray you, as we so often do. And yet you still took unmistakable pride in your people, saying "and in them I am glorified."

Despite countless infidelities, you never stopped loving us. Despite our shame and guilt, you took the time to express your gratitude to the Father for us. All through your priestly prayer, you speak of your disciples as the Father's gift to you. We are not strangers, but "those you have given me."

Over and over in your prayer, you praise God's generosity to you. It is as if that praise overtakes every other thought. You are the Father's unspeakably wonderful gift to us; you also delight in us as the Father's amazing gift to you.

This is our faith: That the eternal Word came among us to save us, to change hearts of stone into hearts of flesh. You squandered the fulfillment of your own human life to give us the possibility of new life. You allowed your existence to be cut short, indeed you drastically limited the possibilities open to your own gifted humanity.

You did all this to devote yourself to our transformation. Unaccountably, in spite of our infidelity, you esteemed us as a priceless gift presented to you by the Father. You did everything for us. The only advantage you reaped was our own salvation.

No friend we may ever have can be as loyal to us as you are, Lord Jesus. How ashamed we feel of the many times we have taken for granted the gracious gift of your presence. The Father sent you into the heart of our daily life. Yet so many of us remain unaware to this day of the way in which you filled and enriched our history. Lovingly and trustfully, you commit us to the Father's watchfulness and care.

Ode to the Trinity

Mystery of the Trinity
Whose loving mutuality
Fills us with adoration.
O mutual generation
Of intimacy
We are called to share.
How can we bear
The awe, the gratefulness
That floods our being
Preformed by your tenderness,
Whispered into your Word divine
Who became our Lord benign
In space and time
In which we travel awkwardly,
Dwarfed by the splendid terror
Of a universe that outshines
The shaken heart, the feeble mind.
Yet only we are called
From eternity into Eternity,
Only our dust is given
To the Word's humanity
As a lasting home,
Transfiguring us
Into unblemished beauty
Before your delighted eye.
Mighty currents of formation
Emanate from you, O Trinity;
A mystical tide
Sweeps invisibly
Through space and time,

Humanity and history,
Inundating all becoming,
Giving rise to countless forms
Of life and matter,
Synchronized in the Father's
Enfleshed eternal Word
In whom we dwell,
Who dwells in us
Lifting us lovingly
Into your mystery,
O Trinity.

9.

To Share My Joy with Them to the Full

John 17:13-16

But now I am coming to you
and I say these things in the world
to share my joy with them to the full.
I passed your word on to them,
and the world hated them,
because they belong to the world
no more than I belong to the world.
I am not asking you
to remove them from the world,
but to protect them from the Evil One.
They do not belong to the world
any more than I belong to the world.

Jesus' joy is the source of our peace and happiness. He promised to share his joy with us. Pained is his sacred heart when we are lured by passing pleasures, by the empty satisfactions of the world in its worldliness, when we forget to alleviate the sufferings of the indigent. All partial joys will deceive us if we do not subordinate them in the deepest joy that Jesus yearns to share with us, so that we may share it with others.

The Lord wants us to spark the flame of that joy in all those who suffer from poverty, pain, disease, and distress. True joy sets us free. It helps us to let go of illusions and to find equanimity.

Joyful Christian living ought to be full of spontaneity, playfulness, liberation, and celebration. Help us, Lord, to draw others lovingly into that luminous circle of Christian joyousness and light.

We recall how thrilled you were by the joy of little children. They need to be embraced and cared for by a family committed to loving one another. In such an atmosphere, children unfold joyously. Parents and others encourage their efforts to crawl, walk, and babble their first words. The joy of performance lights up their little faces.

If only we could keep alive this original delight, this seed of the joy and peace Christ wants to give us, then we would be more ready to say yes when Jesus offers to share his joy to the full. Moments of faith-filled Christian joy are the golden fruit of the abundant outpourings of his love.

Christian joy is as dim as a spent light, it may even be extinguished, if it is not nourished by loving care for others. Care and joy can never be separated. One flows forth from and sustains the other. One cannot last without the other.

"I passed your word on to them, and the world hated them, because they belong to the world no more than I belong to the world."

Christian joy is kept alive by the words Jesus passed on to us. They are a source of faith, hope, and charity. His joy may be hidden in the recesses of our soul. When we suffer, it may seem to disappear under the wounds inflicted on us by the hate of the world. This is because, like Jesus, we do not belong to the world that cannot stand his words.

The radiation of Jesus' joy in our heart and mind may grow dim due to the pain of dissatisfaction we feel when the world in which we live opposes the words Jesus passed on to us. In God's own good time, this suffering may be transformed by grace. Then our joy will emanate from our sharing in Christ's own passion.

We see examples of joy in suffering in the lives of saints and martyrs. In the midst of opposition and persecution, they continued to rejoice in the words of the Lord. People were struck by this paradox of peace in the midst of pain.

Help us, Lord, to read the story of adversity in our own life and that of others as an invitation from you to take part in your sorrowful passion. Give us the grace to radiate your joy under even the harshest of conditions.

In daily life the joyful Christian tries to strike the happy mean between superficial lightheartedness and rigid seriousness, between the person who presses pain behind a false smile and the one who never laughs or enjoys life.

The joy of Christ has nothing to do with raucous wit or an addiction to fun and loud laughter. Neither does it thrive on heaviness of heart. Jesus' joy is a gentle delight in the goodness of life as a gift of the Trinity to us and others.

This kind of joyousness ought to be at the heart of our Christian witness. It ought to light up our tradition. For example, in his book, *De Musica*, Augustine remarks that the truly wise person will from time to time relax the tension of thought and allow its sharp edge to be dulled. The life of the spirit should become as free and fluent as a melody. Mirth is the joyous presence in time of the wisdom of the Eternal. As Proverbs says:

> When he fixed the heavens firm I was there. . . .
> When he laid down the foundations of the
>   earth,
> I was by his side, a master craftsman,
> Delighting him day after day,
> Ever at play in his presence,

At play everywhere in his world,
Delighting to be with the sons of men. (Pv
8:27-29, 31)

Joy loses its fire when people are tempted by a
society that does not care for its own and refuses to
live by the words of Jesus. At times we feel like asking
God to remove us and our fellow Christians from this
world and its evil. Jesus may have felt the same, but
he knew escapism was not the answer. He did not give
in to this temptation, and neither should we. Christians are called with him to live in this world, to heal
its pains, to save souls, to preach the coming of the
reign of God, while not being of this world.

You tell us these things to share your joy with us.
This is the joy we long to experience in the core of
our being in spite of the hate we may incur from
those who resist your ways. We ought not to expect
that fidelity to your ways will gain us admiration in
a world where human ambition and earthly aspiration are ever ascending.

You do not want the Father to remove us from
this world. Rather we are to image your presence in
the midst of it as a reminder of the light and truth
you promised to all who are open to it. You ask only
that the Father protect us from the Evil One, who
constantly tries to seduce us away from you.

Being in the midst of the world, yet not being of
the world, we exemplify a deeper wisdom. The good

things of this earth, the achievements of human history, must be taken up into the glorious form of life you meant for humanity from time's beginning.

Joyous Song

Once a pure melody
Sung by the Trinity
Through its eternal Word,
We were brought forth
In the symphony
Of space and time
To resemble the Divine,
To become a new creation.
As preparation for
The incarnation.
The Logos built itself a home,
The cosmos as his dwelling place.
His lovely face lights up
In stars and trees,
In flowers, birds and bees,
But most of all in people
Who bring to fullness
The form of the Lord.
Their joy is bright,
But in its light
The grave beauty of concern
Balances exuberance of gaiety.
Joyous concern lends nobility
To human life
Resisting the temptation

To play the painful song
Of resignation.
The sacred fight
For people's right
to resist the plight,
The plague of poverty,
The grinding tyranny
of a bureaucracy
That lost its heart
And dreams
In endless reams
Of files and figures.
We bear the weariness
Of people's daily care
Yet keep aware
Of a mystery that moves
The aeons of the evolution,
The labyrinths of history,
The travels of the galaxies,
Radiant with eternity.
We walk the land
Of everydayness
With steady step
Aware that life
Is passing by:
A hurried drive
Along the countryside;
The evanescent sight
Of a sudden flare at night

Of a lonely firefly;
The passing of a bird in flight;
A swan sailing by
In silent beauty
Without a wake
On the surface
Of a soundless lake.

10.

The Consecration of the House of History

John 17:17-19

Consecrate them in the truth;
your word is truth.
As you sent me into the world,
I have sent them into the world,
and for their sake I consecrate myself
so that they too
may be consecrated in truth.

Lord, you pray for the consecration, the making sacred, of our ordinary lives. Consecration is the deepest expression of transformation by the redeeming love of the Father for us through you. He wants us to be transformed in your image as bread and wine are transformed by consecration into your holy body and blood. You want us to flow with this invitation, to yield to the wonder of consecration in our lives.

You ask us in your priestly prayer to dedicate our human formation to the divine mystery of transformation. You answer our plea for consummation by the reconstitution of our life into the image and likeness of God. As the psalmist sings:

> Gates, raise your arches,
> rise, you ancient doors,
> let the king of glory in! (Ps 24:9).

You lift the gates of our faith, hope, and love beyond their boundaries. The ancient doors to our interiority grow higher by virtue of your consecration. Widened by grace, they enable you, the king of glory, to enter into our lives and into all that surrounds and sustains them. The psalmist sings, "How lovely are your dwelling places" (Ps 84:1).

Our dwelling places on earth fluctuate continually through a history of change. You do not stand outside that history, Lord. Your saving will dwells compassionately in the ever unfolding here and now of our life situation. Today we are intently aware of the rapidity of change. Rumors of political and economic alterations hang in the air. Reverberations of instability affect people's daily life, their job security, their family circle. On top of this description, the media bombard us with news of shifts in power and other upheavals all over the globe. Wars, violence, drug abuse, space travels, new inventions, volcanic outbursts, tidal waves—nothing seems stable.

Yet we believe that the history of change in universe, world, and humanity is your dwelling place. How dear has this house of history become to us since you revealed it and made it your house, Lord God of hosts. From the beginning of time, you poured your power not only into hosts of angels but also into hosts of atoms and subatomic particles. You are the Lord of the dance that gave form to the universe and to human life. All that is plays in this graced concert of formation, reformation, and transformation that spans aeons of time.

You disclosed to us through the gifted minds of generations of thinkers, scientists, and artists that at the heart of this changing universe is the mysterious presence of a unitive, formative power, a mystery of formation hidden yet revealed in matter, space, and time. You fill all created beings great and small with your presence and eternal strength. Thus cries the psalmist: "My heart and my body cry out for joy to the living God" (Ps 84:2).

Our heart, our body, our entire organism is an awe-inspiring outcome of the history of an ongoing formative evolution that exults in your creating, consecrating presence in every particle of its unfolding.

In the fullness of time you lift our gates. You make the ancient doors grow higher. You softly enter, king of glory, provided we do not resist your descent into our lives. Like snow flakes in winter or cherry blossoms in spring, your grace drops gently into our world.

Through us you want to enter the house of history in a way that is both consecrating and healing. Consecrated by your presence, you want us to consecrate the world. You ask us to dedicate to the Father all the formation processes and events that make up nature, humanity, and history. You cry out: "Let anyone who is thirsty come to me! Let anyone who believes in me come and drink!" (Jn 7:37-38).

Faith, hope, and love flow out from our consecrated hearts. They nourish rivers of justice, peace, and compassion. They facilitate the abandonment of every human heart to the graced story of formation, reformation, and transformation God has in mind for them.

You want us to dedicate all that exists to your holy mystery. Such dedication is symbolized in people and things traditionally consecrated by priestly sacrifice to the Most High at altars, temples, and holy places.

How generous it is of the Father to invite us to share in his loving act of consecration, to call us to dedicate people, events, and things to his holy presence in creation.

In this part of your priestly prayer, Lord Jesus, you dedicate your own life to the Father. You acknowledge your own power of consecration. You announce forthwith that your suffering and dying will constitute a sacrifice for those entrusted to your care. Your holy passion is thus a priestly consecration that embraces the final consummation to which we are all invited.

You pray: "So that they too may be consecrated in truth." This mysterious truth is none other than a consecration to your word, for you say: "Consecrate them in the truth; your word is truth." God's word is truth. It is his self-communication, the means by which he discloses to us that we will be transfigured by grace, that we will share in Jesus' own self-revelation.

The divine power flows from the Trinity into life, universe, world, humanity, and history. In time it reaches its full expression in Jesus, the incarnate Word of the Father. We adore you, O Lord, as the way, the truth, the life, as containing and expressing the full reality of the divinity.

We ask you to touch and transform the unfolding of our history. Consecrate us in and by the truth that embraces everything. Make us a source of consecration for others. Send us into the world as you have been sent by the Father. "As you sent me into the world, I have sent them into the world."

Help us, Jesus, to be faithful to this mission. Give us the wisdom and strength to pursue excellence in the profession and position assigned to us in this world. Let us become just, peaceful, and compassionate people wherever you place us on the stage of history.

The House of History

Make me yield, my Lord
To the Word
Of consecration,
Of transformation
Of my ways
Melted by the rays
Of your compassion.
May the gates of my life
Lift high their heads,
May the ancient doors
Of mind and heart
Grow higher still,
Open to your will
To enter
The still center
Of this moment,
This shy event
I am in space and time.
Bring victory
To the house of history
In which you dwell.
You are the well
Of the mating dance
Of atomic dust,
This dynamic thrust
Forming the universe
In aeons of time
That follow each other
Like camels
In the deserts

Of empty spaces,
Leaving behind
The traces
Of surging, dying
Planets, stars.
In the end
You descend
Like snow
In winter,
Like blossoms
In spring
Falling softly
From their branches.
You are the spring
Within of living waters
Rising to the brim
Of our hearts
To flow into humanity
Thirsty for consecration
And compassion.

11.

Feeble Echoes
of the Eternal Generation

John 17:20-23

I pray not only for these,
but also for those
who through their teaching
will come to believe in me.
May they all be one,
just as, Father, you are in me and I am in
you,
so that they also may be in us
so that the world may believe
it was you who sent me.
I have given them the glory you gave to me
that they may be one as we are one.
With me in them and you in me,
may they be so perfected in unity
that the world will recognize
that it was you who sent me
and that you have loved them
as you have loved me.

Your prayer holds an invitation. You wish us to dwell in the luminosity of the mystery of mysteries. You pray that we may enter into the greatest mystery: that of the Holy Trinity. You ask us to image among ourselves this life of self-giving love. You want us to recreate it in our loving communion with one another.

Only in you, Lord, can we restore in the Christian community the image of eternal Love. Please, let it be restored. Let it shine forth in humanity. Let us share in the loving communion between you, the Father, and the Holy Spirit. Communion with the Trinity can only be our destiny through the priceless gift of transformation you alone can grant.

We adore the mysterious community of three persons in one divine nature. We marvel at the dynamism of love that forms the inner life of the divinity, the absolute self-giving of this community of three Persons within absolute unity.

In thanksgiving we commemorate the creative outflow of Trinitarian life into time and space. For the same eternal Love that gave form to universe, world, and history comes to life in the womb of Mary. Her humanity, like ours, is called to image in time and eternity the awesome mystery of the Trinity.

You wanted to give us some inkling of the divine life we are to embrace moment by moment. You lifted the veil hiding the Trinitarian mystery that is the wellspring of power emanating into universe and history. This astonishing wealth of generating forces and processes is only a feeble echo of the generation of the Son out of you, loving Father of humanity. Your redeeming love flows through your eternal Word into the creation and ongoing formation of all that was, is, and will be.

Your Spirit moved the writers of the Bible to sing of this mystery:

> Through him all things came into being,
> not one thing came into being
> except through him. (Jn 1:3)

> He is the image of the unseen God
> the first-born of all creation,
> for in him were created
> all things in heaven and on earth:
> . . . All things were created
> through him and for him. (Col 1:15- 16)

The creation of universe and humanity flows forth continually from your Trinitarian life of love. An infinitely deeper creation within this initial generation is the Christian community. You raised it up in the midst of humanity's unfolding as a center of joyous transformation. Within it you assembled compassionately all those redeemed by your beloved Son. This transforming community of Christians is a special emblem of your Trinitarian life. Our unity in Christ has as its model the Trinity, for before the world was formed, he chose us, chose us in Christ, "to be holy and faultless before him in love" (Eph 1:4).

Some beautiful traces of the power of Christian unity may be seen by human eyes. However, its divine source remains veiled from our vision and understanding.

This hiddenness of the sacred source of life and world reminds us of the wonder of your abiding with the people of Israel. Only the gift of faith could disclose to them that the fruits of love spring from you.

The same is true of us, your community of Christians. Together we are called to be assumed with you into the life of the Trinity. Our faith in this silent transformation enables us to see your own life and ours in a whole new light. Our Christian life is disclosed to us as a striking expression in space and time of the mystery of divine love. For you are in us "the image of the unseen God" (Col 1:15).

When we meditate on the priestly prayer as your own last words, we begin to realize how you bring together in it all the past and future treasures that flow from your dwelling among us in the flesh. You pray first for your disciples. May they always accept and cherish your word. Then your prayer embraces each of us. You pray for all "those who through their teaching will come to believe in me." You ask for us, "May they all be one." You grant us an understanding of Christian unity: "May they all be one, just as, Father, you are in me and I am in you."

You then disclose the divine source of our unity: the Trinity. "Just as, Father, you are in me and I am in you." Our union with one another is to be achieved in that image, for it is the divine archetype of Christian unity.

How can we humans be in one another as you and the Father are in one another? Not meant by you is a material or spatial being in one another, like a tree is in the ground, a flower in a vase, or a star in the sky. Through you ours becomes a far more intimate being in one another. It is a spiritual in-being, a meeting of what is deepest in all of us, ultimately what is of you in each of us.

To reach that depth of being in one another, we must go beyond the way we see one another in daily life, or like one another in a jovial, convivial fashion. No matter how good this kind of companionship is, it is a far cry from the unity-in-depth, the true community, you envision for us in your farewell prayer.

Common ways of knowing and liking one another are expressions of everyday vital and functional togetherness. You appeal here, however, to our highest power of loving and knowing. It transcends mere functional knowledge and vital feeling. You then elevate this transcendent power by the gift of your Holy Spirit. Typical of this unique, highest power of mutual love is that understanding and loving permeate one another. Blended together like the rays of a laser beam, they radiate out in unity from the transformed center of our being. When we direct this unique blend of loving understanding or understanding love at other human beings, it appeals to the deepest possibilities you implanted in them. If they are open to the gift, they experience the warmth of an enlightened knowing, of a tender loving, that touches the human heart.

Only this graced blend of spiritual love and understanding allows us to empathize with the divine uniqueness in one another. You call us to imitate in our care for others your care for the Father and the Father's care for you.

Thank you, Lord, for not only painting an ideal picture but for granting us the power of its realization. You enable us to share in the love of the three divine Persons for one another and for humanity. You invite us and enable us to see each other, albeit in a limited human way, with the look with which your Father gazes at you, and by which you, eternal Word, contemplate your Father. You ask us to love one another as the Father loves you, and as you, the Son, loves the Father. Only when you grant us the grace of participating in this divine blend of love and understanding can we mature beyond the oppositions, arguments, and aggravations that threaten to destroy us.

"You are in me and I am in you." You do not mean to encapsulate us in a closed circle of rigid Christians, a gnostic enclave of the elect. You want us to care passionately for justice, peace, and mercy, also for those who live outside our faith community. Twice in this passage you pray for our openness to the world: "So that the world may believe that it was you who sent me. . . . May they be so perfected in unity that the world will recognize that it was you who sent me."

Such selfless care on the part of the Christian community—combined with its own internal loving unity—may move the hearts of people more than anything else. The world suffers under the dissension and distrust, the mutual battles, of a divided and divisible humanity.

Many people of good will strive wholeheartedly for peace, mutual understanding, human encounter, world unity, and loving harmony. Yet human vulnerability in face of the divisiveness that followed the Fall can never be totally overcome by excellent intentions, marvelous slogans, peace marches and conferences, disarmaments, sensitivity training courses and group dynamics alone. All of these efforts can be helpful. They can provide some relief, but not a cure; they should be put into practice insofar as possible, but they will never be sufficient in themselves to overcome our basic disunity.

The need for healing drives our plea for your grace of unity. May this grace manifest itself in our loving Christian community. Enable us to "Take every care to preserve the unity of the Spirit by the peace that binds you together" (Eph 4:3). Let us all be "built up into a dwelling place of God in the Spirit" (Eph 2:22). Then we shall attract others into the light of our community like restless flying creatures leap from the darkness of the falling night into the bright circle of an evening lamp. Let us pray together: Stay with us, Lord, for "it is nearly evening and the day is almost over" (Lk 24:29). Let the Church you love become a community of mutual love and unity so that all people will recognize you living in our midst.

A Shrine in Time

Mysterious Trinity,
Make us dwell
In the clarity
Of the well
Of what is to be.
Do not wait
To recreate
The image
Of divine consonance
In those who believe in you.
Make us a shrine in time
In which you shine
Splendidly.
You are the womb
Of history, the image
Of what humanity
Was meant to be.
What else are we
But feeble echoes
Of the generation
Of the eternal Son,
The archetype, the spring,
Of all becoming,
The hesitant inhabitants
Of your redeeming light,
Elected to be a power of transformation
At the heart of history,
Glowing traces
Of the embraces
Of the divine event,

Rays of the laser beam
Of love divine
In sordid time.
Presence is paralyzed
By profanity.
Finally,
The closed enclave
Of the elect
Empties out
In the teeming streets
Of the divided city
To share with passers-by
Your harmony
O Trinity.

Acknowledgments

I am grateful to my cofounder and present executive director of the Epiphany Association, Dr. Susan Muto, for her beautiful foreword to my book. It was my wish to update and expand the original version of my text without betraying its basic ideas. Both Dr. Muto and my editor at New City Press, Gary Brandl, made excellent editorial suggestions that influenced the final manuscript. Co-editing the text with Dr. Muto's help, led to many improvements that gave form to this new version. I appreciate the invitation of the editor of New City Press to submit my book for publication. Highly valued is the work of the administrative secretary of our Association, Mary Lou Perez. I thank her for her competent typing of the manuscript and for the many other chores she accomplished in the course of preparing this book for publication.

May the Holy Spirit grace all of us with his light, for without this epiphany words remain mere seeds never reaching fertile ground.

1 -855 843-8530
Humane